Olympic
National Park

by Mike Graf

Reading Consultant:
Dr. Robert Miller
Professor of Special Education
Minnesota State University, Mankato

Bridgestone Books
an imprint of Capstone Press
Mankato, Minnesota

Bridgestone Books are published by Capstone Press
151 Good Counsel Drive, P.O. Box 669, Mankato, Minnesota 56002
http://www.capstone-press.com

Library of Congress Cataloging-in-Publication Data
Graf, Mike.
   Olympic National Park / by Mike Graf.
   v. cm.—(National parks)
   Includes bibliographical references (p. 23) and index.
   Contents: Olympic National Park—The Olympic Mountains—People in the Olympic
area—Animals—Plants—Weather—Activities—Safety—Park issues—Map activity—About
national parks—Words to know—Useful addresses—Internet sites.
   ISBN 0-7368-1377-2 (hardcover)
   1. Olympic National Park (Wash.)—Juvenile literature. [1. Olympic National Park (Wash.)
2. National parks and reserves.] I. Title. II. National parks (Mankato, Minn.)
F897.O5 G72 2003
917.97'980444—dc21   2001008094

Editorial Credits

Blake A. Hoena, editor; Karen Risch, product planning editor; Linda Clavel, designer; Anne
   McMullen, illustrator; Alta Schaffer, photo researcher

Photo Credits

Comstock, Inc., 1
Gnass Photo Images/Christian Heeb, 4; Jon Gnass, 6; Charles A. Blakeslee, 14
Tom & Pat Leeson Photography, cover, 10, 12, 17, 18; Gene & Jason Stone, 8, 16

1 2 3 4 5 6 07 06 05 04 03 02

Table of Contents

Washington

4

Olympic National Park

In 1938, the U.S. government set aside part of the Olympic Peninsula as a national park. It wanted to protect the area's forests. It also wanted to protect the rare animals and plants that live and grow in the area.

Olympic National Park is in northwestern Washington. It is part of a peninsula that lies between the Pacific Ocean and the Strait of Juan de Fuca. The park covers more than 1,400 square miles (3,630 square kilometers) of land.

People often say that Olympic National Park is like three parks in one. One area of the park has more than 60 miles (97 kilometers) of coastline. Further inland, there are rain forests and old-growth forests. Old-growth forests are filled with very large trees. Some of these trees are more than 200 years old. The park also includes glacier-capped mountains. Glaciers are slow-moving sheets of ice high in the mountains.

A section of Olympic National Park is along the Pacific Ocean.

The Olympic Mountains

The rocks that make up the Olympic Mountains began to form more than 55 million years ago. Sand washed into the Pacific Ocean and hardened to form layers of rock called sedimentary rock. Around the same time, lava poured out of cracks in the ocean floor. As the lava cooled, it formed into rock.

The surface of the Earth is divided into large sheets of rock called plates. Plates move slowly and rub against each other. Around 30 million years ago, the Juan de Fuca Plate met with the North American Plate. This action created a great deal of pressure. The pressure forced the sedimentary rock and the lava rock to fold upward. These rocks rose to form the Olympic Mountains.

Later, large glaciers carved out the Strait of Juan de Fuca, Hood Canal, and Puget Sound. These waterways separate the Olympic Peninsula from the main part of Washington.

Mount Constance is one of many tall peaks in the Olympic Mountains.

People in the Olympic Area

American Indians have lived on the Olympic Peninsula for thousands of years. They hunted elk, bear, and deer in the area. They fished for salmon. They made canoes from cedar trees. They used cedar bark to make clothing and baskets.

In 1592, explorer Juan de Fuca became the first European to visit the Olympic area. Settlers moved to the area in the mid-1800s. These settlers farmed and began mining and logging on the Olympic Peninsula. In the 1880s, explorers began to map the Olympic Mountains.

In 1909, President Theodore Roosevelt created Mount Olympus National Monument to protect the area's elk herds. Roosevelt elk are actually named after him because he created this park. In 1938, the U.S. government set aside land for Olympic National Park. People then could no longer hunt or log on park lands. In 1953, the area along the Pacific coast was added to the park.

Makah Indians carved drawings on rocks along the Pacific Ocean's coast.

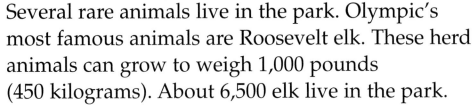

Animals

Several rare animals live in the park. Olympic's most famous animals are Roosevelt elk. These herd animals can grow to weigh 1,000 pounds (450 kilograms). About 6,500 elk live in the park.

Olympic marmots can be found only in the Olympic Mountains. These animals are members of the squirrel family.

Many other animals live in Olympic National Park. These animals include black bears, coyotes, weasels, cougars, river otters, and mule deer. Many frogs and salamanders also live in the park. Bald eagles, woodpeckers, and spotted owls nest in the area's forests. Trout swim in the park's lakes and streams.

Many sea mammals live near and along the park's coastline. These animals include seals, sea lions, sea otters, killer whales, and porpoises. In spring, people can see gray whales swimming along the coast.

Spotted owls are a rare type of bird that lives in Olympic National Park.

Plants

Olympic National Park has several rain forests. The Hoh, Quinault, and Queets rain forests are filled with dense jungles. Sitka spruce and western hemlock trees grow in these areas. Mushrooms, sorrel, giant sword ferns, and carpets of moss grow underneath the trees.

Many large trees grow in the park's rain forests. These trees include the largest Douglas fir, yellow cedar, and western hemlock found in the United States.

Trees in the mountains grow shorter than rain forest trees because of the harsh mountain weather. Krummholz trees only grow about 10 feet (3 meters) tall. Some of these mountain trees are more than 300 years old.

The park also has several types of plants. Sundew plants eat tiny insects. Epiphytes, such as spike moss, lichens, and ferns, grow on other plants. These types of plants are common in rain forests.

Olympic National Park's rain forests are covered with mosses and ferns.

Weather

Olympic's rainy season starts in early fall. It often continues until late spring. The western side of the Olympic Mountains receives up to 150 inches (381 centimeters) of rain and snow each year. More than 200 inches (510 centimeters) of precipitation fall in the high mountains. Most of it is snow.

The eastern side of the Olympic Mountains receives little rain. The height of the mountains prevents most rain clouds from reaching the area. This area receives about 20 inches (51 centimeters) of precipitation each year.

Summers in the park usually are warm and dry. But it can rain or snow any time of year in the mountains. Summer temperatures in the park are between 60 and 80 degrees Fahrenheit (16 and 27 degrees Celsius). Temperatures in the mountains are cooler. Fog blows in from the ocean during summer. The fog helps keep the rain forests damp.

Snow can cover the peaks of the Olympic Mountains year-round.

Activities

The park has more than 600 miles (970 kilometers) of trails. People hike and ride horses on these trails. Some hikers camp overnight in the park. There are more than 900 campsites for people to stay at in the park. During winter, people can cross-country ski or snowshoe on the trails.

People also hike along Olympic's coastline. They can see tide pools there. These small pools contain many interesting types of ocean life such as sea urchins and crabs.

Safety

The weather can change quickly in Olympic National Park. Days can start warm and sunny. But afternoon storms are common. In the mountains, it can snow any time of year. Hikers must prepare for all types of weather. They need to bring rain gear and warm clothing with them on hikes. This clothing will help keep them dry and warm.

People also should hike in groups. Children should hike with adults. These actions will help prevent people from getting lost while hiking.

18

One major concern of park officials is the salmon population in Olympic National Park. Salmon are native to the Olympic Peninsula. These fish migrate to the Pacific Ocean after hatching in mountain streams. Once they grow to adulthood, the salmon swim back to the stream where they hatched. They then spawn, or produce eggs.

The Elwha River runs through the park. People built the Elwha Dam and the Glines Canyon Dam on this river. The dams make it difficult for salmon to reach mountain streams to spawn. The dams block salmon from swimming upstream.

The salmon population has gone down over the years because of the dams. Currently, only 3,000 to 4,000 salmon return to the Elwha River to spawn each year. In the past, about 400,000 salmon migrated up the river. Officials are working on a plan to remove the dams to help increase the salmon population.

Salmon swim upstream to spawn.

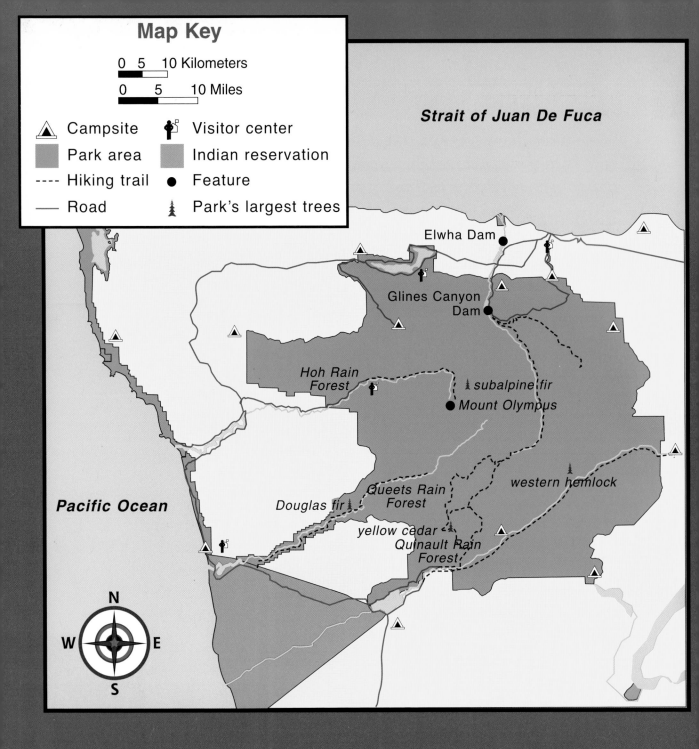

Map Key

0 5 10 Kilometers

0 5 10 Miles

△ Campsite   🚹 Visitor center

▨ Park area   ▨ Indian reservation

---- Hiking trail   ● Feature

—— Road   🌲 Park's largest trees

Strait of Juan De Fuca

Elwha Dam

Glines Canyon
Dam

Hoh Rain
Forest

🌲 *subalpine fir*

● Mount Olympus

western hemlock

Queets Rain
Forest

Douglas fir

Pacific Ocean

yellow cedar

Quinault Rain
Forest

N
W   E
S

Map Activity

Maps have many symbols on them. These symbols help you learn what you can find in the map's area. Park maps show sights you can see, hiking trails, and other features within the park. Learn to use the map's key to understand what's on the map.

What You Need
Ruler

What You Do
1. While visiting a national park, it is a good idea to find out information about the park. Visitor centers will provide this information. Find the symbol for a visitor center in the map's key. Can you find one on the map?
2. There are several campsites for people to stay overnight in Olympic National Park. Locate a campsite on the map. Which visitor center is closest to your campsite? Use your ruler to measure the distance. Use the scale in the map's key to find the distance in miles (kilometers).
3. Olympic's forests are known for having some of the world's largest trees. Look for the symbol of a tree in the map's key. Which large tree is nearest to your campsite?

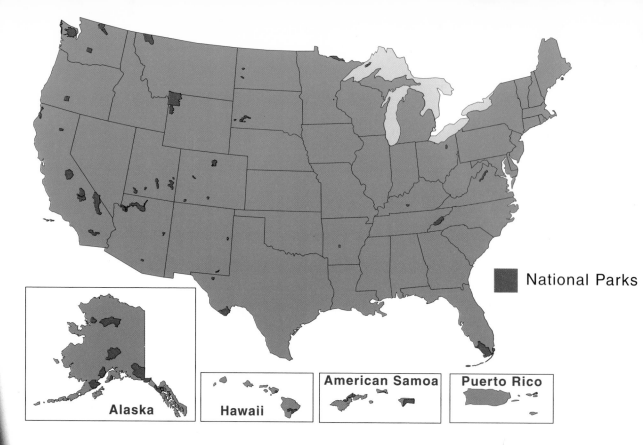

National Parks

Alaska

Hawaii

American Samoa

Puerto Rico

About National Parks

In 1916, the U.S. government formed the National Park Service. It created this organization to oversee all U.S. park lands. The National Park Service runs nearly 400 areas. These sites include recreational areas, natural landmarks, and historic sites such as battlefields. The National Park Service runs more than 50 national parks. These parks protect natural areas such as the Olympic Mountains. People cannot hunt or build on park lands. But they can camp, hike, and view the scenery in these areas.

Words to Know

dam (DAM)—a barrier built across a river or stream to hold back water

epiphyte (EP-uh-fite)—a plant that grows on other plants

migrate (MYE-grate)—to move from one area to another

old-growth forest (OHLD-GROHTH FOR-ist)—a forest consisting mostly of very large and old trees

peninsula (puh-NIN-suh-luh)—a piece of land that is surrounded by water on three sides

plates (PLAYTSS)—the sheets of rock that make up Earth's outer crust

precipitation (pri-sip-i-TAY-shuhn)—the rain and snow an area receives

sedimentary rock (sed-uh-MEN-tuh-ree ROK)—rock that is formed by layers of soil being pressed together

spawn (SPAWN)—to produce a large number of eggs

Read More

Maruca, Mary. *Exploring National Parks.* Tucson, Ariz.: Southwest Parks and Monuments Association, 1998.

Petersen, David. *National Parks.* A True Book. New York: Children's Press, 2001.

Raatma, Lucia. *Our National Parks.* Let's See. Minneapolis: Compass Point Books, 2002.

Useful Addresses

National Park Service
1849 C Street NW
Washington, DC 20240

Olympic National Park
600 East Park Avenue
Port Angeles, WA 98362-6798

Internet Sites

National Park Service—Olympic National Park
http://www.nps.gov/olym
Visitor Guide to the Olympic Peninsula
http://www.olympicpeninsula.org

Index